Bach. Beethoven. Bra

Copyright © 1984 by Amsco Publications,
A Division of Music Sales Corporation, New York
All Rights Reserved

Order No. AM 36476
US International Standard Book Number: 0.8256.2009.0
UK International Standard Book Number: 0.7119.0494.4

Exclusive Distributors:
Music Sales Corporation
257 Park Avenue South, New York, NY 10010, USA
Music Sales Limited
8/9 Frith Street, London W1V 5TZ, England
Music Sales Pty. Limited
120 Rothschild Street, Rosebery, Sydney, NSW 2018, Australia

Printed in the United States of America by
Vicks Lithograph and Printing Corporation

Amsco Publications
New York/London/Sydney

Johann Sebastian Bach

Johann Sebastian Bach

In the lovely old German town of Eisenach, Johann Sebastian Bach was born on March 21, 1685. The house which witnessed his birth still stands.

The boy's father was a violinist and gave the little fellow his first music lessons. Before the age of ten his father died and the child was left an orphan. An older brother, Christoph, then assumed the task of continuing the boy's musical education.

Shortly after this, Bach was forced by reduced circumstances to leave Eisenach and he journeyed to Luneberg where he became a chorister at St. Michaels. Here he was taught the clavichord, the organ and the violin, and also became familiar with the rudiments of composition.

In his great desire to get the best musical training, he often went long distances to hear the foremost musicians of the day. On one occasion he walked two hundred and twenty-five miles to hear the famous organist Buxtehude, play.

Upon the completion of his studies at St. Michaels, he went to Weimar, where he remained for a short time as violinist in the service of the Duke of Weimar.
The scenes of his activities shifted very frequently until the year 1723, which marked his appointment as choir director at the Thomas School in Leipzig, and organist at the church of the same name. It was here that his genius reached its greatest heights and his fame spread throughout the land.

Bach married twice and had twenty children. Two of his sons, Wilhelm and Karl Philipp Emanuel, achieved eminence in the musical world.

Due to the great amount of work he had been doing, Bach's eyesight became impaired and in the year 1749 he became totally blind. From then on his general health declined and on July 28, 1750 he died.

Bach was a very prolific composer and his works are remarkable for their originality. His music is filled with both grandeur and delicacy. Notable among his compositions are the "Well-tempered Clavichord", the Preludes, Fugues, Suites and the Overtures. Many of his greatest creations were written for the church. Included among them are the "B Minor Mass" and the "St. Matthew's Passion."

His music breathes immortal life and will ever remain a monument to his great genius.

Prelude
(No.1, from Well-tempered Clavichord)

J. S. BACH
(1685-1750)

4

Allegro (♩ = 112)

Sarabande
(From the First French Suite)

J. S. BACH

Gavotte

J. S. BACH
(1685-1750)

Invention in F

J. S. BACH

Vivace *Con Allegrezza*

Passepied
(From the Fifth English Suite)

J. S. BACH

Allegretto vivace

Gavotte
(From the Sixth English Suite)

J. S. BACH

D. C. al Fine

Fantasia
C minor

J. S. BACH

Prelude X

J. S. BACH

Fugue X

Two Voices

Gavotte
(From the Third English Suite)

J. S. BACH

Musette

Fine

(una corda)

Gavotte D.C. al Fine

Invention in B flat

J. S. BACH

Poco moderato con moto

Aria
"My Heart Ever Faithful"
(From the Pentecost-Cantata)

J. S. BACH

Andante con moto

Gavotte
(From the Sixth Suite for 'Cello)

J. S. BACH

Prelude VI

J. S. BACH

Allegro moderato

Fugue VI

Three Voices

Solfeggietto

PH. E. BACH
(1714-1788)

Ossia

(a) The closing measure may be played thus

Bourrée
(From the Second Violin-Sonata)

J. S. BACH

Italian Concerto

J. S. BACH

I.

Allegro animato

II.

III.

Ludwig van Beethoven

Ludwig van Beethoven

Ludwig van Beethoven was born at Bonn, Germany, on December 16, 1770. His father had the reputation of being the town drunkard and it was often little Ludwig's task to lead his father home from the tavern. Despite this failing, the elder Beethoven who was a singer, determined that his son should become a musician and taught him to play the violin and piano. He was very severe and the child received frequent beatings as punishment for insufficient practicing.

When Ludwig was twelve, he often played the organ in church, and at this time continued his musical studies under Pfeiffer, Van den Eeden and Neefe.

In 1787 Beethoven went to Vienna where most of the famous musicians of the day lived, and excited much interest by his playing. It was about this time that he experienced his first serious misfortune—the death of his mother and sister within a few months of each other. Being quite alone now, he decided to make Vienna his permanent residence and began his study with Haydn and Albrechtsberger; the latter not seeing much promise in young Beethoven. Many of the nobility became his patrons and foremost among them was Count Waldstein, who regarded Beethoven as the most outstanding of the younger musicians and composers.

Beethoven was now able to earn a comfortable living by playing, composing and teaching and was well on the road to financial independence. Many people considered him eccentric and amusing stories are told of arguments with his housekeeper and neighbors. It is said that once, in a fit of anger, he threw eggs at his housekeeper. However, Beethoven was so evidently a man of genius that people forgave his erratic actions.

In the year 1801, Beethoven began to experience deafness but did not allow this to interfere with his composing. He wrote to a friend concerning this: "I will, as far as possible, defy my fate, though there must be moments when I shall be the most miserable of God's creatures." Year after year the condition grew worse and eventually he could hear nothing of the wonderful music he was writing. It is remarkable that he went on composing and some of his greatest works were written after he became totally deaf. Once at a concert, at which one of his great symphonies was performed, Beethoven could hear none of the applause with which it was received and it was necessary to turn him around to see the audience clapping, for not a sound had he heard.

Beethoven died in Vienna on March 26, 1827, having suffered from the results of a cold which he contracted in 1825.

Beethoven was passionately fond of nature and often composed while walking in the fields. Among his greatest works are the nine Symphonies, the String Quartets, Sonatas, Masses, Concertos, an Opera "Fidelio", and many shorter compositions including songs. It was Beethoven who brought the Symphonic form to its highest degree of development. His music has rare beauty, nobility and incomparable richness of quality.

Bagatelle

L. van BEETHOVEN
Op. 33, No. 6

Allegretto quasi andante

Fuer Elise
(ALBUMBLATT)

L. VAN BEETHOVEN
(1770-1827)

Turkish March
from
"The Ruins of Athens"

Allegretto

L. VAN BEETHOVEN

Minuet in G

L. VAN BEETHOVEN

Ecossaises

(Grade)

L. VAN BEETHOVEN

Rondo

L. VAN BEETHOVEN, Op. 51, No. 1

Moderato e grazioso (♩ = 96)

(a) This appoggiatura should be played, like the *g* in the preceding measure.

Six Variations

on the Duet
"Nel cor più non mi sento"
from the Opera "LA MOLINARA" by Paisiello

L. VAN BEETHOVEN

Andantino quasi Allegretto (♪=160)

THEME

(a) Always strike the grace-note simultaneously with the first accompaniment note, The accent falls, however, not on the appoggiatura, but on the principal note.

VAR.II

(a) Emphasize the left hand slightly here, as it has the principal notes of the melody.

(a) The note G may be played with either the right or the left hand.

(a) Left Hand crosses over the right.(This may be reversed if the player so desires and the notes on the upper staff will then be played by R.H.)

Minuet
from
Sonata Op. 49, No. 2

L. VAN BEETHOVEN

Rondo a Capriccio
(The Rage Over a Lost Penny)

L. VAN BEETHOVEN, Op. 129

Allegro vivace

To Countess Giulietta Guicciardi

Sonata quasi una Fantasia
(Moonlight Sonata)

LUDWIG van BEETHOVEN
Op. 27, No. 2

* The highest part requires a firmer touch than the accompanying figure; and the first note in the latter must never produce the effect of a doubling of the melody an octave lower.

110

II.

Allegretto

Allegretto D.C.

III.

Presto agitato

To Prince Carl Von Lichnowsky

Sonate Pathétique

L. VAN BEETHOVEN, Op. 13

Allegro di molto e con brio

Tempo primo (*Grave*)

Allegro molto e con brio

130

Adagio cantabile

RONDO
Allegro

Johannes Brahms

Johannes Brahms

Johannes Brahms was born on May 7, 1833 in Hamburg, Germany, and was the son of an excellent professional musician, from whom he received his first music lessons. He was a boy prodigy and at the age of ten had already made his debut as a pianist.

In 1853 he toured Germany with the great violinist Remenyi and met Joachim who introduced him to Liszt and Schumann, both of whom greeted him enthusiastically.

As he grew older he performed less and less in public and devoted most of his time to composition.

His music was not readily understood by the musical world of that period and much favorable and unfavorable criticism ensued. However his later works, Overtures, Symphonies, and chamber music have placed him beyond question among the great masters. His songs are recognized as expressing the soul of poetry.

Brahms lived a very calm and quiet life and enjoyed the friendship of the greatest musicians of the time. He died in Vienna on April 3, 1897.

Brahms was often accused of imitating Beethoven, and on the other hand was praised for continuing the master's work. His works have a great purity of form, originality of scheme, and great technical skill.

He has often been pictured seated at a piano, a bulky figure with a flowing beard. As a pianist he was described as a fluent and brilliant performer, though in later years he became somewhat blurred and rather incoherent in his playing.

It has been said that Brahms fulfills the desire for "a composer who, while he maintains and develops the harmonic traditions of the Romantic School, shall even more devote himself to the restoration and evolution of musical structure."

James Huneker, the eminent music critic calls Brahms "the greatest contrapuntist after Bach, the greatest musical architect after Beethoven."

Waltz in A Flat

JOHANNES BRAHMS, Op 39, No. 15
(1833-1897)

Teneramente e grazioso (♩ = 116)

Waltz

JOHANNES BRAHMS,
Op. 39, No. 2

Waltz

JOHANNES BRAHMS,
Op. 39, No. 8

Gavotte

C.W. GLUCK
Transcribed by J. Brahms

Grazioso

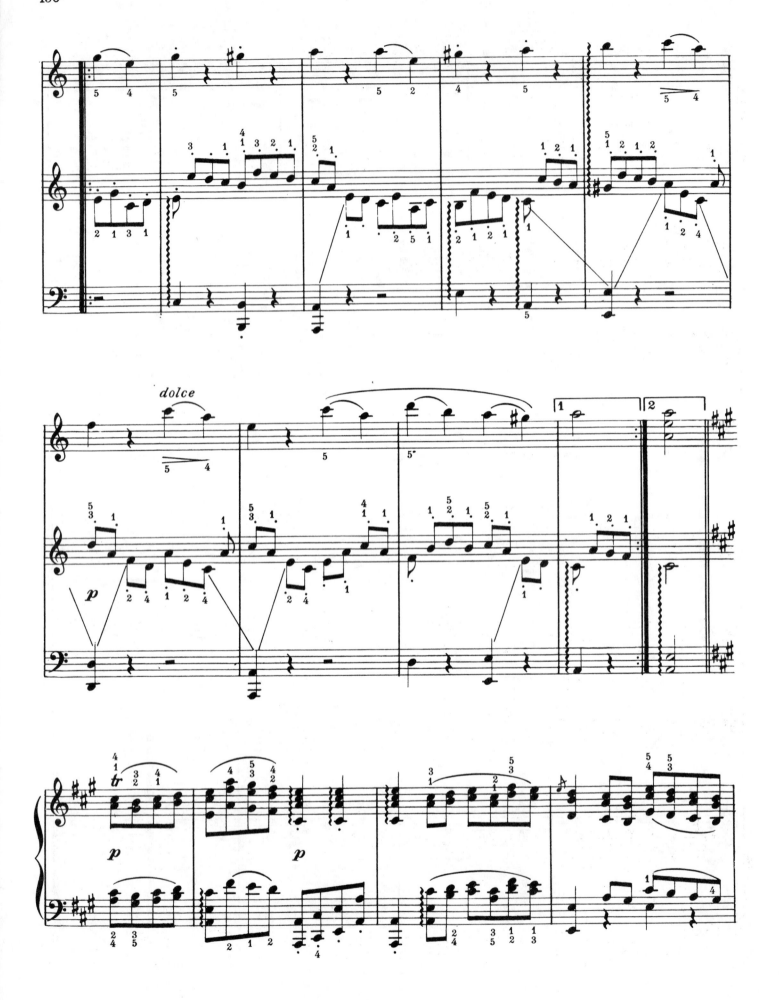

Ballade
After the Scotch Ballad
"Edward"

JOHANNES BRAHMS, Op. 10, No. 1

Andante

Poco più moto

Tempo I

Poco

più moto

Capriccio

JOHANNES BRAHMS, Op. 116, No. 3

Allegro passionato (♩ = 88)

Poco meno allegro

Rhapsodie

JOHANNES BRAHMS, Op.119, No.4

Allegro risoluto

Hungarian Dance
No. 5

JOHANNES BRAHMS

Hungarian Dance
No. 7

Allegretto moderato

JOHANNES BRAHMS

Hungarian Dance
No. 6

JOHANNES BRAHMS

Hungarian Dance
No. 3

JOHANNES BRAHMS

Allegretto

Intermezzo

JOHANNES BRAHMS, Op. 118, No. 2

Andante teneramente